LEMONS

A COUNTRY GARDEN COOKBOOK

LEMONS

A COUNTRY GARDEN COOKBOOK

By Christopher Idone

Photography by Kathryn Kleinman

CollinsPublishersSanFrancisco

A Division of HarperCollinsPublishers

For Jack
and especially for E.V. and R.J.R. with love

First published in USA 1993 by Collins Publishers San Francisco
Copyright © 1993 Collins Publishers San Francisco
Recipes and text copyright © 1993 Christopher Idone
Photographs copyright © 1993 Kathryn Kleinman
Food Stylist: Stephanie Greenleigh
Project Director, Designer, and Illustrator: Jennifer Barry
Editor: Meesha Halm
Design and Production Assistant: Cecile Chronister
Production Managers: Lynne Noone and Jonathan Mills
Library of Congress Cataloging-in-Publication Data
Idone, Christopher.
Lemons:a country garden cookbook/recipes by Christopher Idone:
photography by Kathryn Kleinman.
p. cm.
Includes index.
ISBN 0-00-255165-9
1. Cookery (Lemons) I. Title.
TX813.L4I361993
641.6'4334--dc20 92-43715

Printed in Hong Kong 10 9 8 7 6 5 4 3 2

CONTENTS

INTRODUCTION

Lemons were the basis of my first business venture—a lemonade stand. Like so many kids, my brothers, sister, and I would set little wooden chairs and a small table under a maple tree in front of our house with a big cardboard sign printed in pale, minty green crayon that read "LEMONADE 5 ¢." Our overhead was a galvanized bucket full of ice, a set of tall glasses, and a white enameled pitcher with spout and handle outlined in cobalt blue filled with sweetened lemon juice and water that our mother had prepared. There were no plastic straws and no plastic glasses in those days, nor was lemonade frozen and pink. My younger brother filled the glass with ice, my sister poured, and my second oldest brother and I would hawk to passing cars.

We drank most of it ourselves.

As kids we ate lemons on many occasions. We enjoyed lemon meringue pie for dessert and lemon curd when we visited our grandmother. We squeezed lemon juice on fish and my mother had it with her tea. My father would make his special salad by squeezing a half lemon and olive oil over a mass of greens.

Even so, I never regarded lemons seriously until the late 50's. I was standing on the the terrace of the Count de Cigi's summer residence outside of Siena. We small band of American music students were attending his summer school and all of us had been invited to attend an outdoor concert to hear Casals and Cortot play. In spite of the music, what I remember most was the stone-terraced steps lined with huge ochre planters holding the roots of heady fragrant lemon trees whose perfectly-shaped balls of waxy black-green leaves were laden with mammoth egg-shaped bumpy-skinned lemons weighing down the branches. The smell was so strong, the beauty of the trees so magnificent, the fruit so luscious looking, I was overcome with desire to bite into one.

About this time, I also began seeing lemons in art. In a Dutch still life by Jan van Huysum, fruits and flowers, worms and flies pour over the image; silver urns filled with pomegranates burst with translucent crimson seeds and juice; and salvers of oranges and lemons, still attached to their branches, almost spill out of the canvas.

More subtly, there was the simplicity of Chardin's pyramids of fruits and the charm of Manet's *Luncheon Party* with a partially-peeled lemon dominating the end of the table. Then there were those electric yellows of Braque's bowl of pre-cubist lemons and the pure joy of seeing lemons bounce off the reds and blues of a Matisse.

Best of all, I remember the dark, dense canvas of Bartolommeo Bimbi who recorded botanicals for Cosimo III, the Grand Duke of Tuscany at the end of the 17th century. His painting is a mass of dark green leaves framed by two garden sculptures and a barely visible lattice on top punctuated with some 30 lemons and citrons of various sizes glowing like yellow orbs with ivory tags. Each variety was identified in Bimbi's painterly script at the bottom of the canvas.

Lemons have been with us all along. We know from the tomb paintings in the Valley of the Kings that the Egyptians had lemons, as well as dates, figs, bananas, and pomegranates. In a country where trees were scarce, they were venerated in temple orchards and in the gardens of kings and princes. The Greeks were blessed with not only the olive tree but also the lemon tree to cure and clean, as well as to preserve, decorate, and enliven the foods they ate. The Romans took the lemon from Greece and transported it farther, planting different varieties in France, Spain, Portugal, and North Africa. When the Moors took over most of Spain in the 8th century, they planted lemon orchards throughout Andalusia and lined the paths and doorways of the grand palaces.

Later in the 16th century, the Spaniards carried lemons along with their saplings of figs, apricots, pear, oranges, and apples to the new world. In the suburbs of Mexico City, Cortez divided his famous walled garden with shady walks of lemon and orange trees. In the Spanish church gardens of St. Augustine, Florida, walls made of concrete and sea shells protected the delicate date, fig, pomegranate, orange, and lemon trees.

But interest in citrus trees would not attain its zenith until the 18th century. This was the golden age when venturesome horticulturists, botanists, and architects in France and England were considered men of importance and their primitive laboratories soon became elaborate greenhouses and *orangeries*. These architectural delights had all the amenities of a conservatory. On some estates, the buildings were large enough to house a small grove of orange and lemon trees, which fetched a pretty sum.

At the same time in France, Le Notre, Louis XIV's gardener, brought 3,000 citrus trees from Italy and as far away as the island of Dominica to the *orangerie* at Versailles.

Lemon mania struck the imagination of the low countries as well and they treated citrus with the same reverence as tulips, albeit on a smaller scale. All over Europe, in the summer time, lemon plants were set outside in decorative pots to be admired.

The earliest *orangerie* erected in the United States was at Wye, Maryland, shortly after the American Revolution. Two decades later, Friar Junipero Serra established his first mission in San Diego in 1796; shortly thereafter, 21 mission stations were planted along the Pacific coast. With him, Serra brought lemons, oranges, olives, pomegranates, figs, pears, peaches, grapes, and olives. By the beginning of the 19th century, the San Diego mission was cultivating 200 varieties of fruit trees.

Today lemon trees thrive in backyard gardens from San Diego to San Francisco. When they bloom, their scent is fragrant and heady, their flower as white as moonlight. Commercial California orchards, the backyard counterparts, supply 80 percent of the lemons consumed throughout the country.

The lemon is delightfully versatile. We take it for granted as we peruse the greengrocer's shelf, and without thinking about it, we buy one or two along with a bunch of parsley—sometimes before even deciding what we might be cooking for dinner. Sometimes lemon juice is incorporated into a dish during the early stages of preparation and sometimes it is added after cooking. Even the zest is often an integral part of a recipe and should never be tossed away. The smart cook adds some lemon juice to brighten a sauce, add piquancy to a marinade, and season a mayonnaise. He may also wrap the oily lemon leaves around fish when grilling to keep it moist. The baker fills pie shells with silken, sweet and tart lemon cream, melts the juice with sugar to glaze a cake, and preserves the peel to add delicious perfume to desserts. The good barman rubs a bit of the zest around a martini glass if the imbiber requests a twist . Lemons help disguise the taste of bad water, suppress the sweetness of cola, enliven the flatness of root beer, and make beer taste dryer. For his part, the diner sprinkles the juice over clams, oysters, a piece of fish, a salad, or a slice of ripe melon. Lemons are like salt—they bring out the flavors of food.

GLOSSARY

Varieties: Lemons fall into three categories: Commercial or acid, rough-skinned, and sweet lemons.

Commercial or acid lemons: The most popular and accessible on our greengrocers' shelves is the Eureka. Some say they were supposedly developed in California, but the likelier story is that they were imported from Sicily in the 1870's when Italian immigrants were establishing vineyards in California.

Rough-skinned lemons: Used principally as rootstock for other citrus.

Sweet lemons: The most popular California garden variety is the Meyer, which is occasionally available in markets nationwide. Meyers seem sweeter than the common lemon, but in fact do not contain more sugar, only less acid. Soft yellow and thin-skinned, they are one of the hardiest citrus varieties; they are often grown outside in planters and moved indoors during the cold winters. This variety was grown in Louis XIV's orangerie where ladies of the court sucked on them to keep their lips lusciously red—a practice good for the gums, but not so good for the teeth.

Selecting: Lemons should be firm and oily to the touch. Choose fruit with smooth, brightly colored skin and no tinge of green (a sign of underripeness). Thin-skinned lemons produce more juice than thicker-skinned lemons, which are usually padded with pith, but the zest of the latter is more flavorful and easier to grate or chop.

Storing: Lemons should be stored in an airy basket if you are using them within a few days. They yield more juice when they are at room temperature. If keeping them longer, however, they must be refrigerated. Don't use dried or old lemons to cook with—the taste turns. You can save old lemons and their shells to use with a little kosher salt to shine up copper or to wash your hands with cold water to rid the smells of fish, garlic, and onions.

Juicing: The average lemon yields 2-1/2 tablespoons of juice. The maximum amount of juice can be extracted if you roll the lemon beneath the palm of your hand or drop it in hot water for a few minutes. For me, the best squeezer is the wooden cone-shaped lemon reamer. It fits snugly in the lemon half and extracts all the juice down to the pith. Mechanical and electric juicers are far too cumbersome, the plastic varieties are too complicated, and all of them require constant washing up. When I'm in a rush, I take a half of lemon and squeeze it in one hand and filter the juice through the fingers of the other to catch the pits. If I miss here and there, a pit or two won't kill a recipe.

Slicing: When lemon slices are needed, cut a good portion off the end for juicing and use the center part for nice round slices. When wafer-thin slices are required, use a mandoline.

Eureka Lemon

Zesting: Zest is the yellow, perfumey, outermost layer of skin on citrus fruit. The aromatic oils found in zest are what give so much flavor to foods. The average lemon yields 1 tablespoon grated zest. A potato peeler is the easiest and quickest way of removing the entire zest from a lemon. Be sure to avoid zesting the pale pith found underneath the skin, which is bitter. For best results, peel the lemon from stem end to navel end when needing strips. Each strip can then be sliced lengthwise into needle-thin julienne. When you need the zest diced, take these julienne strips and dice them into fine tiny squares. A zester is a little apparatus that will remove the zest in tiny long shreds. This is best when you want to be decorative. A sharp paring knife works as well, but tends to leave more of the pith on the peel.

Acidity: The acidic value of lemons keeps vegetables such as artichokes, fennel, avocados, and celeriac from discoloring during preparation. Squeezing a little lemon juice in cooking water will keep asparagus or broccoli brilliant green, and cause cauliflower and rice to become whiter. But remember, because of lemons' acidity, use nonreactive pots, pans, and bowls when cooking with them. Use stainless steel, oven-proof glass, ceramic, or porcelain instead and avoid cast iron or aluminum.

Additional terms:

Bottled lemon juice: A poor substitute which bears little resemblence to fresh juice.

Citric acid: Usually made or obtained from lemon juice and used as a flavoring. In salt form, it is called sour salt.

Citron: A fruit similar to the lemon in appearance and structure. The preserved rind is usually candied and used in cakes and puddings.

Citronella: A fragrant grass from southern Asia which yields an oil used in perfumery and as an insect repellent.

Citrus: Any group of soft, thorny trees and shrubs of the rue family grown in warm regions for their edible fruit with firm, thick rinds and pulpy flesh.

Lemon balm: Used in infusions and in liqueurs called *eau des Carmes* or *eau de Mélisse des Carmes*. An Old World mint cultivated for its fragrant lemon-flavored leaves.

Lemon grass: An herb with long grey-green leaves and a scallion-like base essential in Thai, Asian, Indian, and West Indian cooking. Grows in tropical regions such as the West Indies and is the source of an essential oil with a lemony odor.

Verbena: A lemon-scented medicinal plant used in liquors and to perfume certain dishes.

Meyer Lemon

OPENERS

Lemons provide a perfect accent to many of our favorite foods. We squeeze a little juice from the ubiquitous lemon section that accompanies a raw clam or oyster—not so much that they quiver but to perk them up. So too on caviar. Good caviar on toast with just a drop of lemon to enliven those black pearls makes the top layer become milky gray. Magically it suppresses the salt and the true sea flavor comes through. And the acid "cooks" fish when making ceviche.

The soup recipes presented here are variations on classic lemon soups. The cold lemon soup is a version of what is perhaps Greece's most famous soup—avgolemono. Adding mint and serving it icy cold makes a refreshing treat for a hot summer's day. The taste of lemon in the Norwegian salmon soup is more subtle, while it sings forth in the age-old *sopa de limone* from the Yucatan.

Finally, our predilection for pizza is expressed in a crispy dough baked with shaved lemon slices caramelized in the hot oven before being brushed with crème frâiche and punctuated with caviar.

Tapenade in Lemon Shells

Tapenade is as ubiquitous to Provence as a dish of ratatouille.
Make a large batch—it will keep for over a week in the refrigerator.

6 to 8 lemons, to be made into shells
2 cups Greek or Moroccan dry-cured
     black olives, pitted
3 garlic cloves, peeled and crushed
6 ounces canned anchovy fillets, drained and
     patted dry
6-1/2-ounces good quality canned tuna,
     packed in olive oil, drained
1/2 cup capers, drained
1/8 teaspoon white peppercorns

1/8 teaspoon black peppercorns
1 tablespoon green peppercorns in brine, rinsed
     and drained
1/4 teaspoon chopped fresh thyme
2 tablespoons grated lemon zest
1/2 cup lemon juice
1 ounce Cognac (optional)
1-2/3 cup extra virgin olive oil
Salt to taste

Prepare the lemon shells: Cut the tops off the lemons about 1 inch from the stem end. Cut enough of the bottom so the lemons can stand on end. Reserve the tops and discard the bottoms.

Carefully remove the pulp from the lemons with a teaspoon, leaving the skin intact. Pass the pulp through a sieve over a bowl and press down on the pulp gently to extract all the juice. Reserve 1/2 cup of juice for the tapenade and freeze the remainder for another use. Store the lemons shells in a plastic bag and refrigerate until ready to fill.

Place all the ingredients except the olive oil in a food processor fitted with the steel blade. Pulse on and off, adding the oil as you pulse. Season with salt to taste. Do not over-puree. The tapenade should be grainy. Place the mixture in a container, cover, and refrigerate.

When ready to serve, scoop the chilled tapenade into the prepared lemon shells and cap with the tops. Serve individually with toast points or crackers or as a condiment with a tossed green salad. *Yields about 5 cups.*

For a dozen stuffed eggs: Add about 1/4 cup of the tapenade to the cooked yolks and combine. Fill the whites with the mixture.

Alex and Garry's Sopa de Limone

*The Yucatan faces the Caribbean sea so it comes as no surprise
that all the spices and herbs used in this soup are more indigenous to the islands
than to the cooking ingredients we associate with Mexico.*

12 cups chicken stock, homemade or canned
1 sprig mint
8 allspice berries
15 black peppercorns
One 3-inch stick cinnamon
5 whole cloves
6 cumin seeds
2 small heads garlic, sliced in half horizontally
2 small yellow onions, peeled and halved
2 whole chicken breasts, bone and skin left on

1 tablespoon chopped fresh cilantro
1 fresh guero or habañero hot chili pepper, whole
3 lemons, cut into eighths
2 large ripe tomatoes, peeled, seeded, and chopped
Salt to taste
1 lemon, sliced paper thin
Chopped fresh hot chili pepper such as guero or
    jalapeño, seeded, deveined, and finely diced
2 to 3 avocados, peeled and diced

In a large nonreactive soup kettle, bring the stock, mint, allspice, peppercorns, cinnamon, cloves, cumin, garlic, and onions to a boil. Reduce the heat and simmer for 20 minutes.

Add the chicken breasts, cilantro, whole chili pepper, and the cut lemons and continue to simmer until the chicken is cooked, approximately 15 minutes. Remove the chicken and let cool. Skim the soup and strain into a clean kettle. Return the soup to the heat and continue cooking over low heat. When the chicken is cool, remove the skin and bones and shred.

Add the shredded chicken and chopped tomato to the soup and bring to a boil. Add salt to taste. Pour the soup in a warm tureen and float the lemon slices on top. Serve the chopped chili and avocado on the side. *Serves 10*

Cold Lemon Soup with Mint

This soup is a refreshing and cooling version of the Greek classic avgolemono.

4 cups chicken stock, homemade or canned
3 egg yolks
Grated zest and juice of 1 lemon

Salt and cayenne pepper to taste
1 cup heavy cream
2 tablespoon chopped fresh mint

In a nonreactive soup kettle, bring the stock to a boil, reduce the heat, and simmer for 5 minutes.

In a large bowl, whisk the egg yolks. Add the zest, lemon juice, salt, and cayenne. Whisk in the cream and slowly add 2 ladles of hot stock to the egg mixture a little at a time, whisking continuously.

Reverse the process and add the egg mixture to the stock a little at a time, stirring with a wooden spoon. Stir for a few minutes over low heat until the mixture coats the spoon.

Transfer the soup into a large bowl and chill over ice, stirring from time to time to prevent a crust from forming. Refrigerate for at least 2 hours. Serve in chilled soup plates and sprinkle each portion with chopped mint. *Serves 6*

Norwegian Salmon Soup

*Recipes for salmon abound in Scandinavia where the less
meaty tail of this plentiful fish is reserved for a lusty and hearty winter soup.*

*5 cups light fish stock (see p. 23) or a combination
    of half fish stock and half chicken stock*
2 celery ribs, diced
1 celery heart, including the leaves, diced
*2 small leeks, washed and thinly sliced, including
    some of the green*
1 large garlic clove, thinly sliced
1 small fennel bulb, thinly sliced
2 bay leaves
1 sprig thyme
1 teaspoon caraway seeds

*3 ounces tomato paste or 2 large ripe tomatoes,
    peeled, seeded, drained, and chopped*
1 teaspoon lemon juice
Cayenne pepper to taste
*1 pound salmon fillet, skinned and sliced into
    1/2-inch by 2-inch strips*
2 tablespoons small capers, rinsed and drained
1/2 cup sour cream
Grated zest of 1/2 lemon
2 tablespoons chopped fresh dill

In a nonreactive soup kettle, bring the stock, celery, leeks, garlic, fennel, bay leaves, thyme, and caraway seeds to a boil. Reduce the heat, add the tomato paste or chopped tomatoes, lemon juice, and cayenne. Simmer for 15 to 20 minutes or until the vegetables are tender. Add the salmon and capers and simmer for another 5 minutes. Serve in warm soup plates and top with a spoonful of sour cream and a sprinkle of lemon zest and dill. *Serves 4*

Light Fish Stock

Fish stock will bring out the flavor of any fish dish.
Use what you need and freeze the rest for another time.

4 pounds assorted fish bones, including heads, tails,
*   and spines from any non-oily white fish, such*
*   as snapper and bass*
2 medium yellow onions, chopped
3 celery ribs, chopped
3 carrots, chopped

1 teaspoon dried thyme
1 bay leaf
12 black peppercorns
6 sprigs parsley
2 cups white wine
Cold water

Rinse the fish bones under cold running water, making sure the gills have been removed from the head.

In a large nonreactive soup kettle, combine the bones with the remaining ingredients and enough cold water to cover. Bring to a boil and immediately reduce heat to a simmer. Skim the stock and simmer gently for 20 to 30 minutes. Line a strainer with a double thickness of dampened cheese cloth and place over a large pot. Ladle the stock into the strainer and set aside until well drained. Do not press juice from the fish solids. Cool and refrigerate. Stock can be frozen. *Makes approximately 3 quarts*

Lemon Pizza with Crème Fraîche and Caviar

*Pizza is everyone's favorite. This elegant
version can be served as an appetizer or as lunch with a salad.*

Pizza dough:
1/4 cup warm water
2 teaspoons active dry yeast
1/4 cup all-purpose flour
1/2 cup warm water
3 tablespoons olive oil
1/2 teaspoon salt
1-3/4 cups all-purpose flour

Topping:
2 to 3 lemons
Freshly ground black pepper to taste
Extra virgin olive oil
1/2 cup commercial crème fraîche, or 1/2 cup
    sour cream combined with 1/2 cup
    heavy cream, covered, and set for 1 hour
6 ounces good quality salmon roe caviar

Prepare the pizza dough: In a large bowl, combine 1/4 cup warm water, the yeast, and 1/4 cup flour. Cover and set aside for 30 minutes.

Add the remaining water, 2 tablespoons olive oil, the salt, and flour and mix well with a wooden spoon.

Turn the dough onto a lightly floured board and knead for about 15 minutes until the dough is elastic and forms into a ball. Place the dough in a clean bowl rubbed with 1 tablespoon of olive oil and oil the surface of the dough. Cover the bowl with a clean towel and let it rise in a warm place for 1-1/2 hours or until it doubles in size. Punch the dough down and let it rise another 40 minutes.

Preheat the oven to 500 degrees F. If you have a pizza stone, place it on the middle oven shelf. On a heavily floured board, roll out the dough to roughly 12 inches in diameter and about 1/4-inch thick.

Slice the lemons paper thin and remove the pits. Starting 1 inch from the diameter, cover the pizza surface with the lemon slices. Do not overlap. Pepper the lemons and drizzle a little olive oil on top.

Place the pizza on the pre-heated pizza stone or a lightly oiled baking sheet and bake in the middle of the oven for 12 to 15 minutes. After 7 minutes, or when the perimeter of the pizza crust browns and the lemons begins to crisp up, cover the pizza with a sheet of aluminum foil so the lemons do not char. Continue baking until the pizza is browned and the bottom is crisp.

Remove from the oven and place the pizza on a round platter. Let cool for 5 minutes. Using a spatula, spread the crème fraîche over the surface, and sprinkle the caviar on top. Slice and serve immediately.
Serves 4

ACCOMPANIMENTS

The English have an especial fondness for the lemon. They add the juice to butter to spread on tiny cucumber sandwiches which they serve with their tea. They also slice lemons thin and layer them on dense wheat bread to eat with oysters. Best of all perhaps is their lemon marmalade which can rival any Seville orange marmalade, especially when smoothed out with a bit of Scotch.

After colonizing India, Britons took to brightening up their dull diets with curries and chutneys. Indians preserved green or young lemons in mustard, oil, and exotic spices and the English adopted these pungent and pickled lemons, adding their own spin—horseradish and mustard powder.

Moroccans use lemons in much of their cookery; more often than not lemons are preserved in salt. This specialty of provocatively aromatic salted lemons appears in their tagines of chicken, lamb, and fish and is served as well with kebabs and *meshoui*—spit-roasted tender lamb. In the Middle East, lemons are dried until they become black and as hard as stone, while cooks in the homes of Provence string up strips of whole lemon zest to dry and eventually tie them into a bouquet garni to add to a stew or daube.

Lemon Cucumber Tea Sandwiches

These are a nice change from the tried and true cucumber sandwich. Serve them with tea.

Approximately 6 tablespoons unsalted
*   butter, at room temperature*
Grated zest of 1 lemon
1 tablespoon lemon juice with pulp
12 thin slices white or whole wheat bread
1 small cucumber, peeled and thinly sliced
Granulated sugar
Freshly ground black pepper to taste

In a small bowl, cream the butter with the zest and lemon juice.

Evenly spread a light film of butter on each slice of bread. Cover half the bread slices with a thin layer of cucumber.

Sprinkle lightly with sugar and pepper. Cover with the remaining buttered bread slices, trim the crusts, and cut each sandwich into 4 triangles. *Makes 24 tea sandwiches*

Lemon Sandwiches

Serve these with fresh shellfish or smoked salmon, and a glass of chilled, dry white wine.

6 thin slices dense three-grain wheat bread
Approximately 4 tablespoons unsalted butter, at
*   room temperature*
1 lemon, thinly sliced and pits removed
Salt and freshly ground black pepper to taste

Generously butter the bread. Cover half the bread slices with the lemon slices, and season with salt and pepper. Cover with the remaining buttered slices and cut into quarters. *Makes 24 sandwiches*

Bay Scallops with Lemon and Orange

These sweet nuggets only require brief cooking.
If substituting the deep sea variety, cook them a few minutes longer.

2 lemons, preferably Meyer
2 navel oranges
1/4 cup extra virgin olive oil
1 pound bay scallops

Salt and freshly ground black pepper to taste
Pinch of ground cloves
2 small bunches watercress, trimmed,
    washed and dried

Cut 2 strips of lemon zest, finely dice, and reserve. To cut fruit into sections, remove the ends from the oranges and lemons. With a sharp knife, follow the curve of the fruit and cut away the peel and pith. Run the knife between the membranes of each section. Squeeze the membranes over the bowl to catch additional juice and discard. Reserve the sections and juice.

In a large skillet, heat the oil over medium heat. Lightly season the scallops with salt and pepper and a pinch of cloves. When the oil is hot, toss in the scallops and cook for 3 to 4 minutes or until the scallops are opaque. Reserve on a warm plate.

Add 1/2 cup of the citrus juices to the skillet and a sprinkle of olive oil and bring to a simmer. Divide and arrange the watercress and orange and lemon sections on 4 warm serving plates. Spoon the scallops onto the watercress and drizzle the warm dressing on top. Sprinkle with additional pepper and the reserved lemon zest. *Serves 4 to 5*

Squid Salad

Fast cooking is the secret to tender squid.
Serve it with crusty bread and chilled, dry white wine.

3 pounds small squid, cleaned
3/4 cup extra virgin olive oil
Kosher or coarse salt to taste
Juice of 1 lemon
1/2 cup chopped fresh flat-leaf parsley
1/4 teaspoon peperoncino, or to taste
Freshly ground black pepper to taste

Wash and dry the squid thoroughly. Cut the mantles into 3/4-inch rounds and the tentacles into bite-sized pieces. If the tentacles are small, leave whole. Dry on paper towel.

In a large skillet, heat 1/4 cup oil over medium heat. Add the squid and toss in the oil. Cook for 5 to 8 minutes, or until tender. Do not overcook or the squid will toughen. Season with salt and drain in a large sieve. Set aside to cool.

In a large bowl, add the squid and toss with the remaining olive oil, lemon juice, and parsley. Season with peperoncino and pepper. *Serves 4*

Clockwise from bottom: Squid Salad, Bulghur Wheat and Parsley Salad (recipe p. 39), Hot Chili-Spiced Jicama and Carrots (recipe p. 36), Baby Artichoke Salad (recipe p. 36), and Zucchini Marinated with Lemon and Mint (recipe p. 38)

Baby Artichoke Salad

*The pale yellow inner leaves
and hearts of baby artichokes are so delicate and
tender they can be eaten raw.*

*Juice of 2 lemons
36 baby artichokes
2 tablespoons chopped fresh flat-leaf parsley
Salt and freshly ground black pepper to taste
1/2 cup extra virgin olive oil
3 ounces Parmesan cheese*

Fill a large bowl two-thirds full of cold water
and add to it the juice of 1 lemon.

Cut the stem from each artichoke flush
with the base. Snap off the outer green leaves
close to the base. Slice off any spiky tips on the
remaining pale inner leaves and place the artichokes in citric water.

Remove the artichokes from the water
one at a time and with a very sharp knife slice
paper thin and return them to the water. When
all the artichokes are sliced, drain them and pat
dry with a paper towel.

Place the artichokes in a large bowl and add
the remaining lemon juice, parsley, salt, and
pepper and toss with the olive oil. Mound the
artichokes among 6 plates and set aside. Using
a vegetable peeler or cheese knife, shave the
Parmesan into thin sheets over the top of the
salad. *Serves 6*

Hot Chili-Spiced Jicama and Carrots

*The mild ancho and hot pasilla chilies add
just the right spice to these Mexican
crudités. Serve them with a Margarita or
a shot of Tequilla and beer.*

*1 bunch small carrots, washed and peeled
1/2 cup fresh lemon juice or more
3 jicama, peeled
1 dried ancho chili
1 dried pequin or pasilla chili*

Cut the carrots into julienne sticks about 3-
inches long. Place the carrots in a bowl and toss
with half the lemon juice and refrigerate.

Slice the peeled jicama into julienne sticks
3-inches long and place in a bowl. Cover with
the remaining lemon juice, toss, and refrigerate.

If the chilies are not completely crisp and
dry, quickly toast them in a frying pan over
medium heat, making sure they do not burn.
Cool and grind to a powder in a spice grinder.

Place the carrots and jicama on a serving
plate, sprinkle with a little more lemon juice,
and dust with the chili powder. *Serves 6*

Zucchini Marinated with Lemon and Mint

Freshness and simplicity is the mark of a good Italian dish.
What better combination than lemon and mint?

2 pounds small zucchini
1/4 cup plus 2 tablespoons olive oil
2 tablespoons lemon juice

Salt and freshly ground black pepper
*   to taste*
2 tablespoon chopped fresh mint

Wash and trim the zucchini and cut into 1/8-inch rounds. In a large skillet, heat 1/4 cup of the oil over medium heat. Add half the zucchini and sauté until golden on both sides.

Remove with a slotted spoon and drain on paper towels. Repeat with the remaining zucchini slices, adding more oil if necessary. Place the zucchini on a platter and drizzle the remaining 2 tablespoons olive oil and lemon juice over the top. Season with salt and pepper and sprinkle with the mint. Serve at room temperature.
Serves 6

Bulghur Wheat and Parsley Salad

Typically Middle Eastern, this is a healthy and refreshing salad.

1/2 cup bulghur wheat (cracked wheat)
4 cups finely chopped fresh parsley
1 large red onion, finely chopped
3 large tomatoes, peeled, seeded, and diced
1/2 cup finely chopped fresh mint

1 tablespoon grated lemon zest
Juice of 2 lemons
1/2 cup olive oil
Salt to taste

Place the bulghur wheat in a large bowl and add enough boiling water to cover the bulghur by about 1 inch. Set aside for 30 minutes.

In a large bowl, combine the parsley, onion, tomatoes, and mint. Set aside.

Drain the bulghur in a fine sieve, pressing it down to extract the water. Turn the wheat onto a dry towel and squeeze dry. Fluff with a fork to separate the grains. Combine with the herb and vegetable mixture. Mix in the zest and lemon juice. Drizzle the oil over the salad and toss. Season with salt and toss again. Cover and refrigerate until chilled. *Serves 6*

Lemon and Walnut Oil Dressing

This dressing provides an excellent complement for salads that include beets, frisée, endive, radicchio, and other bitter greens.

2 tablespoons lemon juice
Salt and freshly ground black pepper to taste
4 tablespoons walnut oil
2 tablespoons canola oil

In a small bowl, whisk together the lemon juice, salt, and pepper. Gradually whisk in the oils and blend. *Makes approximately 1/2 cup*

Lemon Cream Dressing

This velvety lemon dressing is especially good with sweet tender greens such as bibb, mâche, and butter head lettuces.

Juice of 1 lemon
1/2 teaspoon grated lemon zest
1/4 teaspoon paprika
Salt and freshly ground white pepper
Pinch of superfine sugar
6 tablespoon olive oil
3 tablespoon heavy cream

In a small bowl, mix the lemon juice with the zest, paprika, salt, pepper, and sugar. Whisk in the olive oil, then the cream. Adjust the seasoning if necessary. Store in a covered container and refrigerate. The dressing will keep for a week. *Makes approximately 3/4 cup*

Above: Lemon and Walnut Oil Dressing on left, Lemon Cream Dressing on right

Lemon-Pepper for Raw Oysters, Clams or Mussels

*Most lovers of clams and oysters want the taste
of the sea and eschew heavy sauces. This little embellishment adds just the right kick.*

1 tablespoon grated lemon zest
1 tablespoon cracked black pepper or butcher pepper
1 tablespoon finely snipped chives

In a small bowl, combine the ingredients. Sprinkle a little over shellfish. *Makes 3 tablespoons*

Lemon Butter

This little gem of a sauce is a quick solution for simply prepared fish or green vegetables.

8 tablespoons unsalted butter
1 tablespoon lemon juice
1/2 teaspoon grated lemon zest
Salt and freshly ground black pepper to taste

In a nonreactive saucepan, melt the butter with the lemon juice and zest over medium heat. When the butter melts and begins to sizzle, season with salt and pepper. Remove from the heat and serve over fish, asparagus, or artichoke hearts. *Makes approximately 1/3 cup*

Lemon Marinade

Use this robust marinade to tenderize lamb, pork, chicken, and fish.

1 tablespoon chopped fresh rosemary
1 teaspoon chopped fresh thyme
1 tablespoon red pepper flakes (optional)
3 bay leaves, crushed
4 garlic cloves, chopped
5 strips orange zest, diced
5 strips lemon zest, diced
2 tablespoon lemon juice
1 cup extra virgin olive oil

In a small bowl, combine the herbs and spices with the lemon juice. Gradually add the oil. *Makes approximately 1-1/2 cups*

Moroccan Preserved Lemons

*Preserved lemons are a classic
addition to many Moroccan dishes. The preserving
process takes about three weeks, so make a
big batch and keep on hand.*

6 to 8 lemons
Kosher salt
Paprika
1 teaspoon black peppercorns, crushed
Olive oil
3 garlic cloves, peeled and lightly crushed
3 bay leaves
1 cinnamon stick
Vegetable oil

Cut the lemons in half lengthwise and cut each half into quarters. Remove the visible pits and generously coat the lemon pieces in kosher salt. Set on a pastry rack to drain. Set aside for 24 hours—they will become soft and limp.

Pat the lemon pieces with a clean kitchen towel and arrange in layers in a sterilized glass jar. Lightly sprinkle each layer with a little paprika, crushed pepper, and olive oil. Add the garlic clove and a bay leaf at every third level and the cinnamon stick in the middle. Cover the lemons with a combination of half olive and half vegetable oil. Seal and refrigerate.

In about 3 weeks the pickled lemons will be soft, mellow, and ready to eat. Keeps for 6 weeks after marinating. Serve in tagine dishes, grilled fish, and curry dishes. *Makes 1 quart*

Lemon-and Herb-Spiced Olives

*Spiced olives are the perfect
accompaniment to aperitifs and wine, or
served with an alfresco lunch.*

4 cups unpitted green olives, or a combination of
    Nicoise and Moroccan green and black olives,
    drained of brine
Approximately 1 cup virgin olive oil
2 tablespoons chopped fresh rosemary
1 tablespoon chopped fresh thyme
2 whole red chili peppers, julienned
4 large garlic cloves, peeled and crushed
6 white peppercorns, crushed
6 black peppercorns, crushed
Zest of 1 lemon, julienned
1 teaspoon mustard seeds, crushed

Lightly crush the olives with the back of a chopping knife on a cutting board. This will cause them to absorb more of the flavors.

In a small sauté pan, heat 1/2 cup olive oil over medium heat. Add all the ingredients except the olives and warm for about 3 minutes or until the herbs and spices release their aromas.

Place the olives in a quart jar or ceramic container. Add the remaining olive oil or enough to cover the olives. Cool, seal, and refrigerate. Olives will keep for months. *Makes 4 cups*

MAIN COURSES

Lemons are a natural complement to meats like chicken and veal. A half lemon is essential to a fried cutlet as the juice counteracts the richness of fried foods. The zest, when chopped and combined with garlic and parsley, adds zing in sautéed veal chops with gremolata. A whole lemon, when pierced with a fork and stuffed in a chicken, imbues the roasting bird with delicate lemon flavor and keeps the breast moist. When preserved in the Moroccan fashion, it can be incorporated into tagines of lamb or chicken, or served as an accompaniment to chicken and fish dishes. As a base for a marinade, its juice adds piquancy to the grilled chicken sandwich.

Lemons also provide a perfect accent to fish. Paired with fish dishes, its tartness acts as a natural foil to the salty-sweetness of most sea creatures. The zest adds pizzaz in the pan-seared salmon with pesto and thin slices dusted with bread crumbs atop baked cod create a crisp, fragrant crust.

Its uses are boundless, but lemons are meant to enhance these main courses, not to overpower them.

Moroccan Tagine with Prunes and Preserved Lemon

*Almost always made with lamb, tagines from Morocco contain
an array of intoxicating spices which came there en route to Europe from the Far East.*

Tagine:
*3 pounds lean lamb, neck or shoulder, trimmed
    and cut into 2-inch cubes*
1/4 cup olive oil
Salt and freshly ground black pepper to taste
3 medium yellow onions, finely chopped
1/2 teaspoon tumeric
1 teaspoon ground ginger
1/2 teaspoon ground cinnamon
1/4 teaspoon cayenne pepper
1/8 teaspoon saffron threads, crushed
*4 cups chicken stock, homemade or canned, or a com-
    bination of half lamb and half chicken stock*
2 bay leaves
3 sprigs parsley
3 medium potatoes, peeled and cut into 1/2-inch slices

6 small carrots, peeled and cut into 2-inch pieces
3 small turnips, trimmed, halved, and cut into thirds
18 dry prunes, soaked in warm water
12 preserved lemon sections (see p. 45)

Harissa sauce:
*1 teaspoon harissa, or more depending on personal
    taste, or substitute hot red chili paste*
1/2 cup broth from the tagine
1 tablespoon virgin olive oil
1 tablespoon lemon juice
1 tablespoon chopped fresh cilantro

Couscous:
1-1/2 cups cold water
1/2 teaspoon salt
1-1/2 cups instant couscous

Pat the lamb dry with paper towel and set aside. In a large heat-proof casserole, heat the oil over medium heat. Salt and pepper the lamb. When the oil is hot but not smoking, brown the meat on all sides until golden. Remove the meat from the casserole and set aside.

Add the onions and sauté for 2 to 3 minutes or until they begin to give up their juices. Add the ground spices and saffron and cook for another 3 minutes or until the onions are soft and the spices give off their aromas. Stir occasionally. Add the stock and bring to a boil. Add the lamb, bay leaves, and parsley, and reduce the heat to a simmer. Cover slightly and cook for 40 minutes or until the meat is almost

tender, stirring from time to time. Taste for seasoning. (The tagine can be made a day ahead at this point.) Add the potatoes, carrots, and turnips, cover, and simmer for 20 minutes or until the vegetables are almost tender. Add more stock or water if there is not enough liquid.

Prepare the harissa sauce: In a small sauce pan, whisk the harissa with the hot broth over high heat and boil for 1 minute. Stir in the remaining ingredients and remove from the heat. Reserve in a heated sauceboat.

Prepare the couscous: In a medium sauce pan, bring the water and salt to a boil. Stir in the couscous, remove from the heat, cover and set aside until all the liquid is absorbed, approxi-

mately 10 minutes. Fluff up the grains with a fork just before serving.

While the couscous cooks, drain and add the prunes and preserved lemon to the tagine.

Cook an additional 10 minutes. Mound the couscous onto a serving platter or warm plates and serve the tagine on top. Serve the harissa sauce on the side. *Serves 6*

Sautéed Chicken Paillard with Lemon

Although you don't cook with it, a splash of fresh lemon juice brightens this chicken dish.

2 whole chicken breasts, boned, skinned and excess fat removed
1 cup coarsely ground bread crumbs
1 teaspoon chopped fresh rosemary
1 teaspoon chopped fresh thyme
1 tablespoon finely chopped fresh parsley
Salt and freshly ground black pepper to taste
2 eggs
1/4 cup olive oil
2 lemons, halved

Cut each breast in half and place each half between 2 pieces of waxed paper. With a rolling pin, lightly pound the chicken until it is about 1/4- to 1/8-inch thick.

Combine the bread crumbs with the herbs, season with salt and pepper, and spread on a large flat plate. Set aside. In a small bowl, lightly beat the eggs.

In a large skillet, heat half the oil over medium heat. Dip the chicken in the egg and then dust with the bread crumb mixture. In-crease the heat and lay 2 paillards in the pan, making sure they do not overlap. Cook for about 2 minutes on each side or until both sides are golden, shaking the pan so they do not stick. Remove from the pan and drain on paper towel. Add more oil if necessary and cook the remaining 2 paillards. Place the paillards on 2 warm individual plates with half a lemon on the side.
Serves 4 or 2 generously

Lemon Fritters

These tart-centered fritters can be served just after a meal or as a delicious foil for game, fish, and curry dishes.

3 large lemons
1/8 teaspoon baking powder

Batter:
2 eggs, separated
1 cup all-purpose flour
1/4 teaspoon salt
1/2 teaspoon baking powder
1 tablespoon unsalted butter, melted
1/2 cup milk
Vegetable oil, for frying
Salt to taste

In a pot of lightly salted water, add the lemons and baking powder. When the water comes to a boil, drain the lemons and refresh under cold water. Remove the ends of the lemons, cut in half lengthwise, and then cut each half into quarters. Remove the pits and set aside.

Prepare the batter: In a large mixing bowl, whisk the egg yolks and sift in the flour, salt, and baking powder. Add the butter and milk. In a medium bowl, whisk the egg whites with a pinch of salt until stiff. Fold into the batter.

In a deep-fryer or deep saucepan, heat the oil to 375 degrees F. Coat the lemon pieces with the batter a few at a time and fry until golden. Remove the lemon pieces with a slotted spoon and drain on paper towels. Lightly season with salt. *Makes about 24 fritters*

Roast Lemon-Stuffed Chicken

Stuffing the chicken with lemon and herbs perfumes the flesh and keeps it moist.

One 4-1/2 to 5-pound chicken, neck and wing
    tips reserved
Kosher salt and freshly ground black pepper to taste
1 large lemon
2 large sprigs thyme

1 1/2 tablespoons olive oil
1 whole head garlic, unpeeled, cut in half
horizontally
1 cup chicken stock, homemade or canned
1 tablespoon lemon juice

Preheat the oven to 425 degrees F.

Remove the fat from the cavity of the chicken and salt and pepper the cavity. Prick the entire surface of the lemon with a fork and place the lemon and thyme in the cavity of the bird. Truss the bird and rub the skin with the oil. Season the exterior of the chicken with salt and pepper and place on its side in a baking dish. Scatter the neck, wings, and garlic alongside the chicken.

Place the baking dish in the center of the oven and roast for 20 minutes. Baste the chicken, turn on to the other side, and roast another 20 minutes. Baste again, turn the chicken breast side up, and roast for an additional 20 minutes (for a total of 1 hour).

Reduce the heat to 375 degrees F. and baste again. Continue roasting until the juices run clear when pierced in the thigh joint with a sharp paring knife, approximately 15 minutes.

Transfer the chicken and garlic halves to a warm platter. Turn off the oven and place the chicken in the oven with the door ajar for 10 minutes or longer while you make the sauce.

Spoon off the excess fat from the baking dish and place the dish over medium heat. Add the stock and lemon juice. Bring to a boil and scrape up the brown bits from the bottom of the dish. Reduce the heat and simmer for about 5 minutes or until the sauce begins to thicken.

Carve the chicken and arrange on the platter with the garlic halves. Strain the sauce through a fine sieve and pour into a warmed sauceboat. *Serves 4 to 6*

Veal Chop with Gremolata

*Usually served with the Milanese dish Osso Buco, gremolata adds
zing and zest to almost any veal dish.*

Gremolata:
1 tablespoon finely chopped lemon zest
2 small garlic cloves, finely chopped
*2 tablespoons finely chopped fresh
    flat-leaf parsley*

Veal:
4 tablespoons olive oil
*4 loin veal chops, cut 3/4-inch thick with
    the bone in*
Salt and freshly ground black pepper to taste
1/2 cup chicken stock, homemade or canned
1 teaspoon lemon juice
3 tablespoons unsalted butter

Combine the gremolata ingredients in a small bowl and set aside.

In a large skillet, heat the oil over high heat. Season the chops with salt and pepper and place them in the pan. Cook the chops over high heat for 5 minutes on each side or until golden but still pink in the center. Place the chops on a serving platter and place them in a warm oven.

Pour off the oil from the skillet and return to the heat. Add the stock and lemon juice. Bring to a boil and scrape up the browned bits from the bottom of the pan. When the stock begins to thicken, swirl in the butter.

Remove the chops from the oven and place them on warm serving plates. Pour the sauce through a strainer over the chops. Sprinkle each chop with a little gremolata and serve immediately. *Serves 4*

Grilled Chicken Sandwich with Red Pepper Rouille

The hot pepper rouille adds just the right smoky sharpness to this main meal sandwich.

1-1/2 cups of marinade (see p. 43)
6 large chicken breasts, boned, skinned, and excess
  fat removed

Hot Pepper Rouille:
1/2 yellow sweet bell pepper, charred, peeled,
  deveined and seeded
3 hot red cherry peppers, charred, peeled, deveined
  and seeded, or 1 tablespoon hot pepper flakes
3 large garlic cloves, peeled
2 egg yolks
1 cup olive oil
Salt and freshly ground black pepper to taste
Grated zest of 1/2 lemon
Juice of 1/2 lemon

Sandwich:
6 sourdough sandwich rolls, or 2 long sourdough
  baguettes divided into thirds
1 small head frissé, washed and dried
18 red cherry tomatoes, washed and stems removed
18 yellow cherry tomatoes, washed and
  stems removed
12 baby artichokes, trimmed, cooked, and
  cut in half
2 tablespoons olive oil
1 teaspoon lemon juice
Salt and freshly ground black pepper
1 tablespoon finely chopped fresh flat-leaf parsley

Prepare the marinade and set aside. Place the chicken breasts between 2 pieces of wax paper and flatten lightly. Place the chicken in the marinade, cover, and refrigerate for 2 hours or more.

Meanwhile, prepare the rouille: Char the peppers over an open gas flame or charcoal grill. When cool enough to handle, peel away the blackened skin. In a food processor, combine the bell pepper, cherry peppers, and garlic. Pulse until pureed. Add the egg yolks and puree. Gradually add the oil and process until the rouille is the consistency of mayonnaise. Add the salt, pepper, lemon zest, and juice, and pulse until blended. If the rouille is too thick, add 1 tablespoon of boiling water and pulse. Place the rouille in a container, cover, and refrigerate until ready to use.

Prepare a charcoal grill or preheat the broiler. Remove the chicken from the refrigerator and pat dry. Discard the marinade. When the grill is hot, season with oil. Grill the breasts over a medium-hot fire until lightly charred and golden, approximately 5 minutes on each side. Set aside to keep warm. Slice the rolls in half and toast on the cut side. Coat the rolls with some of the rouille. Place some frisée and a chicken breast on the bottom half of each roll. Top with the other half of the roll.

In a small bowl, combine the cherry tomatoes and artichokes with the oil and lemon juice, season with salt, pepper, and parsley and toss. Spoon the vegetables on the side of the sandwich.
Serves 6

Pappardelle with Lemon and Asparagus

No peeling, no fuss. When pencil asparagus are available at the market, this makes for an easy pasta supper.

1 pound pencil-thin asparagus, approximately 32
    asparagus
2 tablespoons unsalted butter
1 cup heavy cream
1 pound fresh or dried pappardelle

2 tablespoons extra virgin olive oil
Juice of 1 lemon
Freshly ground black pepper to taste
Zest of 1 lemon, cut into julienne
Grated Parmesan cheese for serving

Cutting on the diagonal, trim the tough ends of the asparagus. Cut the asparagus into 3 or 4 even pieces on the diagonal. In a nonreactive kettle of lightly salted boiling water, cook the asparagus for 2 minutes or until just crisp. Blanch in cold running water and drain.

In a sauce pan over medium heat, melt the butter and cream. Allow to cook at a low simmer.

Cook the pappardelle in the kettle of salted boiling water until al dente and drain well. While the pasta is boiling, heat the oil in a large skillet and add the blanched asparagus. Add the hot cream mixture and fold in the lemon juice. Season with pepper.

Add the drained pasta to the sauce and toss well. Divide among 4 or 5 warm soup plates and sprinkle with juilienned zest. Serve with grated Parmesan cheese. *Serves 4 to 5*

Spaghetti with Clams, Lemon and Parsley

Pasta with olive oil is a natural pairing. The addition of water to the oil lightens the sauce.

4 dozen small littleneck clams
1 sprig thyme
1 bay leaf
1/2 small yellow onion, thinly sliced
One 2-inch strip of lemon zest
1/2 cup dry, white wine
1 pound dried spaghetti

Sauce:
1 cup olive oil
4 garlic cloves, minced
Zest of 1 lemon, finely diced
1 cup chopped fresh parsley
Salt and freshly ground black pepper
    to taste

Scrub the clams, place them in a steamer basket, and set them in the freezer for 10 minutes. (This will cause the clams to open faster.)

Bring a large kettle of salted water to a boil for the spaghetti.

In a large steamer, add the thyme, bay leaf, onion, lemon zest, and white wine. Bring to a boil and place the basket of clams in the steamer. Cover and cook until the clams open. Remove the clams to a large bowl as they open—not all the clams will open at once. Cover the bowl slightly and set aside. Carefully pour off the steamer liquid through a strainer and reserve 1 cup. Moisten the cooked clams with the remaining liquid.

Cook the spaghetti for about 12 minutes or according to package directions.

While the spaghetti is cooking, place the oil and 1/4 cup water in a deep saucepan, set over medium heat, and cover. When the oil begins to warm, add the garlic and lemon zest and simmer for 5 minutes. Carefully add the clam liquid and bring to a simmer for about 3 minutes. Add the parsley and turn off the heat.

Drain the spaghetti in a colander, making sure not to shake off all the moisture. Return the spaghetti to the kettle and place over low heat. Pour in the clam sauce, season with salt and black pepper and toss well.

Divide the spaghetti among 4 warm pasta plates and surround the plate with the clams.
Serves 4 to 5

Baked Cod with Tomatoes, Zucchini and Lemon

For best results, rely on a mandoline for thin slices of onion and zucchini and sheets of lemon slices.

3 medium yellow onions, peeled and thinly sliced
6 tablespoons good olive oil
1 tablespoon chopped fresh thyme
Kosher salt and freshly ground black pepper
3 pounds cod fillet, or substitute scrod or halibut
2 to 3 medium tomatoes, blanched, peeled, and
    thinly sliced
3 small zucchini, thinly sliced
1 cup light fish stock (see p. 23), or substitute
    homemade or canned chicken stock
1 cup dry white wine
2 lemon, sliced paper thin
1-1/2 tablespoons unsalted butter
1/2 cup fresh bread crumbs
2 tablespoons chopped fresh flat-leaf parsley

Preheat the oven to 350 degrees F. In an oven-proof baking dish, make a layer of onions on the bottom. Drizzle with half the oil and the thyme, and season with salt and pepper. Place the fish over the onions and layer the tomatoes and zucchini. Pour in the stock and wine to fill the dish halfway. Sprinkle the remaining oil and thyme on top. Cover with the lemon slices.

In a small skillet, melt the butter over medium heat and toast the bread crumbs until lightly golden. Mix with the parsley and season with salt and pepper. Dust the surface of the lemons with the bread crumbs. Bake in the oven for 30 minutes or until the fish is opaque and slightly springy to the touch. *Serves 8*

Pan-Seared Salmon with Lemon Cilantro Pesto

This recipe from Jon Gilman, Taste Caterers, New York, is characteristic of their spirited menus.

Pesto:
3 cups fresh cilantro
1/2 cup fresh mint
1 cup toasted almonds
1/2 cup grated pecorino cheese
Zest and juice of 4 lemons
3/4 cup olive oil
Salt and freshly ground black pepper to taste

Salmon:
1 tablespoon curry powder
1 teaspoon chili powder
2 teaspoons kosher salt
1/2 tablespoon flour
16 tablespoons (2 sticks) unsalted butter, melted
Four 6-ounce salmon fillets, skin and bones removed

Prepare the pesto: In a food processor with a steel blade, blend all the ingredients except the oil, salt, and pepper, until fine. Drizzle in the olive oil and season with salt and pepper. Set pesto aside.

Preheat the oven to 400 degrees F. Heat a cast iron skillet on the stove for 8 minutes over medium-high heat. Mix the curry, chili powder, salt, and flour in a shallow dish. Pour the melted butter into a shallow dish and dredge the salmon in the butter and dust with the flour mixture. Place the salmon in the hot skillet and sear for 2 to 3 minutes on each side. Remove from the pan and bake on a baking sheet for 5 minutes. Fillets should be served rare to pink. Place the fillets on warm plates and drizzle with pesto. Serves 4

SWEETS

The lemon lover likes the flavor of puckery citrus to shine through his desserts as much as the chocoholic wants the sensation of luxurious, rich chocolate to underscore his sugar. One taste is light and tangy, the other rich and earthy. Though rarely paired together, candied lemon dipped in melted chocolate is an exquisite combination.

A little zest of lemon in a pastry shell, scone, sorbet, or ice cream adds just enough citric oils to hint of lemon flavor. A bit of juice in fruit salads or a squeeze over strawberries or raspberries with a bit of sugar intensifies the flavor and excites the palate.

When making lemon desserts, I suggest using Meyer lemons when available. Unfortunately, they only occasionally reach the market place. Meyers are bright yellow, delicate tasting, and have a more complex perfume and a sweeter flavor than the Eureka lemon. The difference is similar to using a true key lime for a pie. That doesn't stop us from making the pie when a regular lime will have to do. It's a different taste—but still a good pie.

Lemon juice freezes well, so save the juice when you have squeezed too much. When you have enough, make a souffle, sorbet, tart, or curd.

Left: Lemon Curd (recipe p. 66)

Lemon Curd

*Although lemon curd is typically made with butter,
I prefer to omit the butter in this lighter version. Serve lemon curd with scones, muffins,
toast, or fresh berries, or use as a tangy filling in a prebaked tart shell.*

4 egg yolks, at room temperature
1/2 cup granulated sugar

Grated zest of 1 lemon
1/2 cup fresh lemon juice

In a small stainless steel bowl or in the top of a double boiler, whisk the egg yolks and sugar together. Add the zest and whisk in the lemon juice. Set over a pot of simmering water and whisk constantly until the mixture thickens, approximately 10 minutes.

Remove from the heat and strain the mixture through a fine sieve into a glass or ceramic container. Cover with plastic wrap and refrigerate until cool. *Makes approximately 1 cup*

Meyer Lemon Marmalade

Meyer lemons grow in California gardens from L.A. to San Francisco.
They are sweeter, more flavorful, and more perfumey than the usual store-bought variety.
Buy them when you see them. For lemon lovers, this marmalade will
rival any orange marmalade from Seville.

1 pound Meyer or Eureka lemons
1 pound small sugar cubes

1 ounce good malt Scotch whiskey

Wash and scrub the lemons. Place them in a large pot and cover with cold water. Bring to a boil, reduce the heat, and simmer for 30 minutes or until the flesh can be easily pierced with a knife. Drain and set aside to cool.

Cut the lemons crosswise into very thin slices. In a nonreactive heavy pot, combine the lemon slices and sugar and place over low heat. Cook, stirring until the sugar cubes dissolve. Bring to a boil, stirring often so the lemons do not scorch on the bottom of the pot. Cook until the syrup reaches 200 degrees F. and the lemons are translucent. Skim off any foam, add the Scotch, and continue cooking for approximately 5 minutes or until the marmalade coats the back of a spoon.

Spoon the marmalade into sterilized jars and seal according to manufacturers directions. Boil the jars in a water bath for 15 minutes and let cool. Seal and refrigerate. The marmalade will keep about 1 month. *Makes about 3 cups.*

Lemon Scones

*At teatime, serve these lemon-scented scones with curd or
lemon marmalade and a little clotted cream if you are a traditionalist.*

2 cups all-purpose flour
2 tablespoons granulated sugar
2 tablespoons baking powder
Zest of 2 lemons, finely diced
3/4 cup currants

2 tablespoons unsalted butter
2 eggs, lightly beaten
1/2 cup heavy cream
1 egg beaten with 1 tablespoon cold water,
    for egg wash

Preheat the oven to 400 degrees F. Sift the flour, sugar, and baking powder into a large mixing bowl. Add the zest. Cut the butter into bits and rub it into the flour by hand or with an electric mixer. Combine the eggs and cream and mix into the flour mixture. Fold in the currants. Do not overmix.

Divide the dough in half. On a lightly floured surface, roll out the dough 1/2-inch thick. Cut the scones with a 2-inch round cookie cutter. Repeat with the remaining dough. Press any leftover dough together and continue cutting out the rounds until all the dough is used.

Place the scones 2 inches apart on 2 baking sheets and chill for 15 minutes. Brush the tops of the scones with the egg wash and bake for 15 to 20 minutes or until golden brown. *Makes about 24 scones*

Lemon Squares

Lemon squares are addictive confections that can be eaten at any time of the day.

Crust:
3-1/2 cups all-purpose flour
1/4 cup confectioners' sugar
1/4 teaspoon salt
28 tablespoons (3-1/2 sticks) unsalted butter,
*   cut into bits*

Filling:
6 large eggs
3 cups granulated sugar
1 tablespoon grated lemon zest
1/2 cup lemon juice
2/3 cup all-purpose flour
1 teaspoon baking powder
Confectioners' sugar for dusting

Preheat the oven to 350 degrees F. In a large bowl, sift together the flour, sugar, and salt. With a pastry blender or 2 knives cut the butter into the mixture until it is the consistency of cornmeal. Press dough into a baking sheet 17-inches by 12-inches by 1-inch. Bake for 15 minutes or until crust is lightly browned.

In a large bowl, beat the eggs until blended and beat in the sugar. Add the zest and gradually fold in the lemon juice. Sift the flour and baking powder into the egg mixture and blend until smooth. Pour the mixture over the crust and bake for 25 minutes. Cool in the pan on a rack. Using a sharp knife, carefully cut into squares and dust with confectioners' sugar. *Makes 4 dozen squares*

Mrs. Teddy Donahue's Lemon Cake

There is a reason for packaged cake mixes and this is it!

1 box Duncan-Hines Lemon Supreme cake mix
One 3-1/2 ounce box jello instant lemon pudding
1/4 cup lemon juice
4 eggs
1/2 teaspoon lemon extract
2/3 cups canola oil

Glaze:
1/4 cup lemon juice
1 teaspoon grated lemon zest
1/2 teaspoon lemon extract
1 cup confectioners' sugar

Preheat the oven to 350 degrees F. Prepare the cake: In the bowl of an electric mixer, add the cake mixture and instant pudding and set aside.

In a measuring cup, add the lemon juice and enough cold water to make 2/3 cup. Add the eggs, lemon water, and lemon extract to the dry ingredients and combine. Pour in the oil, and beat at medium speed for 6 minutes or until smooth.

Lightly oil a Bundt pan, pour in the mixture, and bake for 45 minutes or until the top is golden and the cake is springy to the touch. While the cake is baking, prepare the glaze: In a small bowl, whisk the lemon juice, zest, lemon extract, and confectioners' sugar until smooth. Set aside.

When the cake is done, cool down for 5 minutes, invert, and unmold. Using a poultry needle or toothpick, pierce the top of the cake with 1-inch deep holes. Spoon the glaze over the cake and cool. Serve with fresh berries. *Serves 10*

Lemon Meringue Pie

For ultimate lemon meringue pie, the crust must be flaky,
the filling, tart and sweet, the meringue, sweet but not cloying,
and the texture, gossamer with a little chew. This is it!

Pastry Tart shell:
1 cup all-purpose flour
1 tablespoon granulated sugar
1/8 teaspoon salt
1/2 teaspoon grated lemon zest
8 tablespoons unsalted butter, cut into bits
Approximately 1-1/2 tablespoons cold water

Meringue:
3 egg whites (reserved from the custard)
1/2 teaspoon lemon juice
1/2 teaspoon vanilla extract
3/4 cup plus 1 teaspoon granulated sugar

Lemon Custard:
Grated zest of 2 lemons
1/3 cup lemon juice (approximately 2 lemons),
*   strained*
3 eggs, separated (save whites for the meringue)
1 egg
1/3 cup sugar
2 tablespoon heavy cream
1/3 teaspoon cornstarch
5-1/3 tablespoons unsalted butter
*   (approximately 1/3 cup), cut into bits*

In the bowl of an electric mixer, sift the flour, sugar, salt, and add the zest. At low speed, mix in the butter until the mixture is the consistency of cornmeal. Add the water and mix until the pastry holds together. Wrap the pastry in plastic wrap and let it rest for 30 minutes.

Preheat the oven to 375 degrees F. On a lightly floured surface, roll out the dough into a 12-inch circle about 1/8-inch thick. Roll up the pastry loosely around the rolling pin then unroll it over a 9-inch pie pan. Ease the pastry into the pie pan and lightly press into the contours of the pan. Cut the pastry about 1/2 inch beyond the edge of the pan and crimp the edges with a fork. Cover with the plastic wrap and refrigerate for 15 minutes or until ready to bake.

Bake for 20 minutes or until lightly golden. Remove and let cool. The pie shell can be made ahead and frozen at this point.

Prepare the lemon custard: In a nonreactive bowl, combine the zest and the lemon juice. Set aside.

In a nonreactive saucepan, beat the egg yolks and egg with the sugar until thick and lemony in color. Combine the cream and cornstarch in a small bowl and add to the egg mixture. Whisk in the lemon mixture and place the pan over medium heat. Add the butter bit by bit, whisking constantly until it coats the whisk. Pour the custard into a bowl and whisk again. Cover with plastic wrap and chill. (The custard will keep for 2 weeks.)

Prepare the meringue: In the bowl of an electric mixer, beat the whites until frothy. Beat in the lemon juice and vanilla extract and slowly increase the speed. Gradually add 3/4 cup sugar and beat until the meringue forms glossy, stiff peaks. Mound the meringue over the filling and swirl into peaks.

Sprinkle with the remaining 1 teaspoon of sugar and bake for 15 minutes or until the meringue is lightly browned. Let cool. *Serves 8*

Frozen Lemon Soufflé with Melted Blueberries

When blueberries are in season, this deep blue sauce is a refreshing accompaniment.

Soufflé:
1-1/2 teaspoons unflavored gelatin
1/2 cup lemon juice plus 1/2 teaspoon
3 eggs, separated
2/3 cup sugar
Grated zest of 1 lemon
1 cup heavy cream

Melted Blueberry Sauce:
1 pint fresh blueberries
1/2 cup granulated sugar
2 lemons slices

Prepare the soufflé: In the top of a double boiler, dissolve the gelatin with 1/2 cup lemon juice. When juice is warm and the crystals have dissolved, set aside.

In a large bowl, beat the yolks with 1/3 cup sugar until the mixture is thick and lemony in color. Fold the lemon mixture into the yolks, whisk, and return to the double boiler. Set over medium heat and continue to whisk for about 8 minutes or until the mixture coats the back of a wooden spoon. Fold in the zest, cover with plastic wrap, and set aside to cool.

In the bowl of an electric mixer, beat the whites until frothy. Beat in the 1/2 teaspoon lemon juice and slowly increase the speed. Gradually add the remaining sugar and beat until the meringue forms glossy, stiff peaks. Thoroughly blend a large spoonful of the beaten whites into the cooled lemon mixture.

Whip the cream. Fold the remaining meringue into the lemon mixture with a rubber spatula and then fold in the whipped cream. Do not overblend—streaks of white should show through. Fold the mixture into a 1-1/2 quart soufflé dish and set in the freezer for 2 hours.

In the meantime prepare the sauce: In a nonreactive saucepan, combine the berries with the sugar and lemon slices. Place over medium heat and cook until the berries give off their juices but keep their shape, approximately 5 minutes. Discard the lemon slices and serve warm or at room temperature with the soufflé. The soufflé may be served directly from the freezer or left to soften in the refrigerator 1/2 hour before serving. *Serves 4 to 5*

Lemon Ice Cream

*This silky and tangy cream is a refreshing end to any meal and can be glamorized
with fresh fruit and fruit sauces for a fancy dinner.*

3 lemons
2/3 cup sugar
1 cup half-and-half

5 egg yolks
3 cups heavy cream

Pare the skin of 1 lemon into long strips. Place the peel, sugar, and half-and-half in a non-reactive saucepan over medium heat. Stir with a wooden spoon until the sugar dissolves. Heat until the mixture begins to boil. Remove from the heat and let cool for 15 minutes.

In a medium bowl, whisk the yolks until thick and lemony in color. Gradually add the half-and-half mixture, whisking constantly. Pour the mixture into the saucepan and cook over medium heat, stirring constantly, until the mixture coats a spoon. Strain the mixture through a fine sieve into a large bowl.

Grate the zest of the remaining 2 lemons and add to the mixture. Stir in the cold heavy cream and allow to cool.

Juice the lemons and measure 1/2 cup of strained lemon juice into the cool mixture and reserve any additional juice for another use. Chill. When the mixture has cooled, freeze in an ice cream maker according to the manufacturer's directions. *Makes 1 quart*

Granita di Limone

A quick and easy icy dessert for a hot summer's day.

1 cup sugar
3 cups water

1 cup lemon juice
2 sprigs mint

In a nonreactive saucepan, combine the sugar and water and bring to a boil. Stir until the sugar dissolves. Reduce the heat and simmer for 5 minutes.

Remove from the heat and pour in the lemon juice. Bruise the mint and add to the mixture. Let cool.

Strain the mixture into 2 flat pie pans. Set in the freezer for 1/2 hour and scrape the granita with a four-tined fork. Return to the freezer for 2 more hours, scraping the granita every half hour or until it is a flaky slush.

When ready to serve, grate the granita with a fork into 6 chilled small goblets. *Serves 6*

BEVERAGES

Lemon zest and lemon juice found their way into liqueurs and drinks long before we added a twist to the martini. Lemon was the first flavoring used in soda water back in 1840 and it is still the most refreshing additive in spite of the fruit-flavored waters so popular today.

Venerated throughout history for its medicinal and healing qualities, lemons are steeped in vodka for the popular Italian digestif Limoncello and combined with barley water for an old-fashioned restorative used to treat invalids in the 19th century. Essential oils from lemon balm and lemon verbena infused with spririts give us *eau de Carmes* and brewed with hot water give us the aromatic tea tisane.

Lemons are a major ingredient for the barman who makes good cocktails with a flair, and for Americans, nothing beats fresh lemonade on a hot summer's day. I prefer the *citron presse*—the juice of half a lemon, ice, and soda or water, with or without a lump of sugar—available at every corner bar and cafe in France.

Lemon Barley Water

Lemon Barley water is a 19th-century beverage used as a digestive and considered to be a kidney cleanser as well. Today, it is sold in bottles like soda pop in England.

1/2 cup pearl barley, washed and drained
1/8 teaspoon salt
Whole peel of 1 lemon
Juice of 1 lemon
Sugar syrup to taste (see p. 91)

Wash the barley in cold water and strain. In a nonreactive saucepan, add the barley, salt, and lemon peel, and 10 cups cold water. Bring to a boil, reduce the heat, and reduce the mixture by half, stirring from time to time so the barley does not scorch the pan. Strain the liquid and discard the barley. Add the lemon juice and sugar syrup to taste. Place the mixture in a sterilized bottle. Cap and chill. *Makes 4 drinks*

Horse's Neck I

This once popular drink got its name from the spiral of lemon hanging over the edge of the glass. It looked like the mane of a horse.

Peel of 1 lemon, cut into a spiral
5 ounces ginger ale
2 or 3 drops Angostura bitters

Place the peel in a highball glass and hook the end over the rim of the glass. Fill the glass with ice cubes and pour in the ginger ale and bitters. Stir. *Makes 1 drink*

Horse's Neck II

Peel of 1 lemon, cut into a spiral
1-1/2 ounces Cognac
5 ounces soda water

Place the peel in a highball glass and hook the end over the rim of the glass. Fill the glass with ice cubes and pour in the Cognac and soda water. Stir. *Makes 1 drink*

Lemon Grog

This is a great cold weather drink—to cheer you up, warm you up, or help nurse a cold.

1 teaspoon sugar
Juice of 1/2 lemon
1-1/2 ounces dark rum or whiskey

Place the sugar in a warm mug. Add the lemon juice and rum and pour in 5 to 6 ounces boiling water. *Makes 1 drink*

Lemonade de Luxe

This is lemonade with a punch.

1 ounce vodka
6 ounces lemonade

Serve vodka over ice and lemonade. Stir and serve. *Makes 1 drink*

Lemon Shandy

This old timers' drink is a summer refresher popular among sailors at seaside taverns throughout the British Isles.

Juice of 1/4 lemon
4 ounces soda water
12 ounces chilled ale or lager

In a chilled Pilsner or beer mug, add the lemon juice and soda. Slowly pour in the ale and serve. *Makes 1 drink*

Lemon Shandy II

2 ounces lemonade
12 ounces chilled beer

Pour the lemonade into a chilled Pilsner or beer mug. Slowly pour in the beer and serve. *Makes 1 drink*

Limoncello

Limoncello is a thick, syrupy liqueur popular along the Amalfi Coast and Capri.

1 quart vodka	*2 cups water*
Whole peel of 6 lemons	*3/4 cup sugar*
1 sprig lemon verbena	

Combine the vodka, lemon peel, and verbena in a dark glass or ceramic container. Cover loosely and keep in a cool place or refrigerator for 7 days.

In a medium saucepan, stir cold water with the sugar over medium heat until it dissolves. Bring to a boil and cook for 5 minutes. Let cool.

Strain the vodka through a fine mesh sieve into a clean container. When the syrup is cool, add to the vodka. Cover and keep cool. Steep in a cool place for another week and pour into sterilized bottles. Cap and store in the refrigerator. When serving, freeze the liqueur at least 6 hours ahead. *Makes approximately 1 liter*

For a beautiful presentation, freeze the limoncello in a block of ice laced with fresh yellow roses: Open up the top of a 1-quart milk carton and rinse thoroughly. Set the vodka bottle filled with limoncello in the center. Place long stemmed yellow roses standing up around the bottle. Pour enough distilled water to reach the base of the bottle neck. Place the container in a deep freezer, making sure it sits flat on its base, or else the block will be crooked. It will take about 24 hours to freeze completely. When ready to use it, remove the block from the freezer and tear off the cardboard. Display in a deep tray. You can also try filling the ice block with sliced lemons.

Nicolashka

*This is a Russian drink with an
accompanying ritual—A slice of lemon that has
been sprinkled with sugar and
powdered espresso is bitten and eventually chewed
and swallowed while imbibing
shots of icy cold vodka.*

1 lemon, sliced paper thin
Superfine sugar
Instant espresso
Frozen vodka

Dust a lemon slice with sugar and espresso.
Accompany with shots of frozen vodka.
Makes 1 drink

Bray's Lemonade

*A friend of mine who grew up in
Brownsville, Texas invented this, explaining,
"It's hot down there and I wanted the
lemon taste 'til the end."*

2 cups sugar
*3 cups lemon juice, approximately 12 large
    lemons, strained*
3 cups soda water
Mint sprigs for serving

Prepare the simple syrup: Place the sugar and 4
cups cold water in a saucepan and bring to a boil
over high heat, stirring with a wooden spoon
until sugar dissolves. Continue to boil for 5
minutes and remove from the heat. Cool and
refrigerate in a covered container. Simple syrup
keeps for 3 to 4 weeks refrigerated.

In a large pitcher, combine 1-1/2 cups
lemon juice with 1 cup simple syrup and 3 cups
cold water. Mix and pour into ice cube trays
and freeze.

When ready to serve, combine the remaining lemon juice and simple syrup and 3
cups soda water or ice water and mix. Pour over
lemonade ice cubes. Add a mint sprig and
straw. *Makes 6 drinks*

INDEX

ACKNOWLEDGEMENTS

I want to thank all those friends and colleagues who helped and cheered this little book on, especially Linda Donahue, Cheryl Mercer, Maryanne Page, Bob Bray, Dina Nargil, Mr. & Mrs. Theodore Donahue, Gary Farmer, Alex Galindo, Jon Gilman at Taste, Gary Regan at the Spotty Dog Bar and Market Diner in N.Y.C., Rico Puhlmann, and Tom Dillow for the juice of eleven lemons.

Also, to the wonderful group at Collins, San Francisco, I want to thank Lena Tabori for including me as part of this series, Meesha Halm for being a fast and exact editor, Jenny Barry for her esthetic eye when designing this book, Kathryn Kleinman for her photography, and Stephanie Greenleigh for food styling ...thank you all.—Christopher Idone

Photography Acknowledgements:
Collins and the photography team would also like to thank Michaele Thunen, prop and floral stylist; Michele Miller and Dimitrios Spathis, photo assistants; Pat Brill, food stylist assistant; Sara Slavin, props; Ellen Georgiou; Koulis and Sophie Pontikis; and Ken and Yvette Poisson from Les Poisson Antiques, San Francisco. Special thanks to: Tail of the Yak for the Italian cake stand, Berkeley, CA; Jerri Goldberg for the Antique Lemon Print, Lyons LTD., San Francisco, CA; Bill Fujimoto from Monterey Market, Berkeley, CA; Ana Le Blanc; Betty Jane Roth; and Jody Thompson Kennedy.

Approximate Metric Conversions

Liquid Weights

U.S. Measurements	Metric Equivalents
1/4 teaspoon	1.23 ml
1/2 teaspoon	2.5 ml
3/4 teaspoon	3.7 ml
1 teaspoon	5 ml
1 dessertspoon	10 ml
1 tablespoon (3 teaspoons)	15 ml
2 tablespoons (1 ounce)	30 ml
1/4 cup	60 ml
1/3 cup	80 ml
1/2 cup	120 ml
2/3 cup	160 ml
3/4 cup	180 ml
1 cup (8 ounces)	240 ml
2 cups (1 pint)	480 ml
3 cups	720 ml
4 cups (1 quart)	1 litre
4 quarts (1 gallon)	3 3/4 litres

Dry Weights

U.S. Measurements	Metric Equivalents
1/4 ounce	7 grams
1/3 ounce	10 grams
1/2 ounce	14 grams
1 ounce	28 grams
1 1/2 ounces	42 grams
1 3/4 ounces	50 grams
2 ounces	57 grams
3 ounces	85 grams
3 1/2 ounces	100 grams
4 ounces (1/4 pound)	114 grams
6 ounces	170 grams
8 ounces (1/2 pound)	227 grams
9 ounces	250 grams
16 ounces (1 pound)	464 grams

Temperatures

Farenheit	Celsius (Centigrade)
32°F (water freezes)	0°C
200°F	95°C
212°F (water boils)	100°C
250°F	120°C
275°F	135°C
300°F (slow oven)	150°C
325°F	160°C
350°F (moderate oven)	175°C
375°F	190°C
400°F (hot oven)	205°C
425°F	220°C
450°F (very hot oven)	230°C
475°F	245°C
500°F (extremely hot oven)	260°C

Length

U.S. Measurements	Metric Equivalents
1/8 inch	3 mm
1/4 inch	6 mm
3/8 inch	1 cm
1/2 inch	1.2 cm
1 inch	2.5 cm
3/4 inch	2 cm
1 1/4 inches	3.1 cm
1 1/2 inches	3.7 cm
2 inches	5 cm
3 inches	7.5 cm
4 inches	10 cm
5 inches	12.5 cm

Approximate Equivalents

1 kilo is slightly more than 2 pounds
1 litre is slightly more than 1 quart
1 meter is slightly over 3 feet
1 centimeter is approximately 3/8 inch